Watchman Responsibility

Praise for Watchman Responsibility

**Rev. Dr. Laura Shannon McDaniel, Global Director
Uptick, "A Generation of Jesus-Shaped Leaders"**

With prophetic urgency, Pastor Lenita issues a clarion call for *every believer* to wake up and sound the alarm as the Watchmen on the Wall. If you are deeply concerned over what is transpiring in our nation and around the world, you need to *take action now* and read this book to gain spiritual wisdom and practical steps to pray with your God-given authority. Stand with us and declare the Word of God against the *"coordinated attacks on our nation and execute God's judgment against them and the agendas of nations who seek destruction."* Remember, we fight *from* a place of victory, not toward it!

**Juin Killingsworth, Maryland State Coordinator
National Day of Prayer**

For such a time as this, Lenita Reeves' Watchman Responsibility is being released. Rev. Lenita has yielded to the voice that God has spoken to her to alert covenant believers and church leaders to watch and pray for America. God's Word is unfolding, and His watchmen should read this book!

**Bishop Nii Quaofio, Action Worship Center:
Dansoman, President, Godfactor Summit**

In a world plagued by turmoil, uncertainty, and spiritual darkness, the call to stand as watchmen on the wall has never been more crucial. Rev. Lenita Reeves' timely book, *Watchman Responsibility*, issues a prophetic warning to believers everywhere: arise, pray with fervor, and take your stand against the enemy's insidious plans. Through prophetic insight and divine guidance, Rev. Reeves exposes the spiritual battles raging around us, from the orchestrated attacks on nations to the looming economic and cultural crises. With clarity and conviction, she navigates the complex web of spiritual warfare, urging believers to claim their God-given authority and intercede for their nations and communities. Let us join the ranks of other faithful believers and stand against the forces of darkness! Heed the call dear reader, and align yourself with God's purposes. May this book be a catalyst for spiritual awakening and proactive prayer in your life.

Bishop Adongo Joseph, Senior Pastor, Prosperity City Chapel International, Accra, Ghana

In this book, by prophetic direction, Pastor Lenita Reeves gives a deeper insight into our responsibility as watchmen and the reasons why we should watch and pray. There is no better time to wake up to our godly responsibility as watchmen than now! The happenings around the world lend credence to the fact that indeed the enemy is up in arms against God's children and His nations. Get ready for destiny-changing encounters as you explore this book!

Watchman
Responsibility

Winning the End-Time Warfare
to Stand Watch and Pray
Effectively

Lenita Reeves

Purpose House Publishing

Dedication

To those who have stood with me in the midnight prayer watch.

"The basis for our New Testament watching is not whether we are prophets, it's anticipation of the Lord's return. Jesus said, 'Be always on the watch, and pray that you may be able to escape all that is about to happen, and that you may be able to stand before the Son of Man'"
(Luke 21:36 NIV).

Contents

ISBN: 978-1-957190-15-0

Scripture quotations marked (AMP or AMPC) are taken from
the Amplified Bible Copyright 2015 by The Lockman
Foundation. Used by permission. All rights reserved.

Scripture quotations marked (CJB) are taken from the
Complete Jewish Bible, Copyright © 1998 by David H. Stern.
Used by permission. All rights reserved.

Scripture quotations marked (ERV) are taken from the Easy-to-
Read Version, Copyright © 2006 by Bible League International.
All rights reserved.

Scripture quotations marked (KJV) are taken from the Holy
Bible, King James Version (Public Domain).

Scripture quotations marked (MSG) are taken from THE
MESSAGE, copyright © 1993, 2002, 2018 by Eugene H.
Peterson. Used by permission of NavPress. All rights reserved.

Scripture quotations marked (NIV) are from the New
International Version, Copyright © 1973, 1978, 1984 by Biblica.

Scripture quotations marked (NKJV) are taken from the New
King James Version®, Copyright © 1982 by Thomas Nelson.
Used by permission. All rights reserved.

Scripture quotations marked (NLT) are taken from the Holy
Bible, New Living Translation, copyright © 1996, 2004, 2015 by
Tyndale House Foundation.

CHAPTER 1: ANOINTING OR RESPONSIBILITY?

"God opens their ears and impresses them with warnings to turn them back from something bad they're planning, from some reckless choice, And keep them from an early grave, from the river of no return." – Elihu in Job 33:16-18 MSG

It was midnight Thursday night, January 27, 2024, crossing over into the dawn of Friday, January 28, 2024, and that night was different. Women and men joined me to sacrifice their late hours in prayer so others could sleep in peace—but that wasn't what was different. I have been leading midnight prayer for over two decades, and other faithful believers have joined me in that prayer watch over the years. What was different that night was what God showed me and the heightened level of evil associated with it.

He opened my spiritual eyes, and in the spirit realm, I saw a judge's gavel come down from heaven, smash down on Earth, and execute judgment. Then, like a fist pressing into my chest, pinning me against a wall, I felt a weight of evil, a cloak of darkness I'd never experienced. I saw anti-God nations coming together

1

to collaborate and conspire to pass evil decrees, policies, and acts that would not favor the people of God and attack nations that were in alignment with Israel. It was like they were passing an act of war, but their motive was hatred for Israel and God.

The vision continued.

I saw the same nations planning to attack America during the time of the presidential election, getting closer to November 2024, capitalizing on the media frenzy that would surround former President Trump in the election. The plan was to attack America while she was in transition and vulnerable during the election season.

In the vision, they wanted to send a message to America that she was no longer a superpower. "Aha," they said, "we are the superpowers now." Like King David said, "They also opened their mouth wide against me, *And* said, "Aha, aha! Our eyes have seen *it*" (Psalm 35:21 NKJV).

This was not the first time God had revealed terrorist attacks in the making during midnight prayer. But that night was different—what I saw was raging, collaborative, coordinated, and a level of evil I had never seen before. Now, I realize the evil behind what I saw is the same evil behind the anti-Israel, anti-God, antisemitic, anti-anything-Judeo-Christian sentiment we are seeing on college campuses and in response to Israel defending herself after October 7, 2023. I have never seen America (and Americans) be so anti-Israel. It is a drastic departure from our nation's history. Behind the scenes, there's a dark power at work. "For our struggle is not against flesh and blood, but against the rulers, against the authorities, against the powers of this dark world and against the spiritual forces of evil in the heavenly realms" (Ephesians 6:12 NIV).

Beloved, nations are imagining all kinds of evil, and it's not only about the Jews. They chant, "Today we come for the Saturday people (Jews); tomorrow we come for the Sunday people (Christians)." It's an attack against the Western world, its associated Judeo-Christian values, and God's sovereignty and ultimate rule over all nations. It's the beginning of the end, where the antichrist will take the stage. The battle will rage over Israel and its temple, where the abomination of desolation will be erected (Matthew 24:15, Daniel 9:27, 11:31, 12:11).

As I write, Israel has been at war since October 7, 2023—over ten months. We can't ignore this because the Scripture says, "when these things begin to come to pass, then look up, and lift up your heads; for your redemption draweth nigh" (Luke 21:28 KJV).

Remember the parts of the vision.

1. First, nations came together to collaborate and conspire to pass evil decrees, policies, and acts that would not favor the people of God and attack nations that were in alignment with Israel. It was like they were passing an act of war, but their motive was hatred for Israel and God.

Little did I know that although Israel constitutes a little over one-tenth of one percent of the world's population, they receive 70% of the United Nation's (UN) complaints, and those complaints have increased in 2024. Fifty-six of the fifty-seven members of the Organisation of Islamic Cooperation (OIC) are also UN member states, with forty-eight of those being Muslim-majority countries.[1] The OIC states that it is the second largest organization in the world after the UN, with a membership of 57 states spread over four continents.[2] Moreover, on Tuesday, July 23, 2024, Beijing brokered a Hamas and Fatah agreement to ban together for a unified Palestinian rule while the Israel-Hamas war continued[3]— decrees, acts, and laws were

---

[1] Organisation of Islamic Cooperation, "Member States," accessed August 2, 2024, https://www.oic-oci.org/states/?lan=en.

[2] Organisation of Islamic Cooperation, "History," accessed August 2, 2024, https://www.oic-oci.org/page/?p_id=52&p_ref=26&lan=en

[3] "Hamas and Fatah sign unity deal in Beijing aimed at Gaza governance," Aljazeera.com, July 23, 2024, Accessed July 31, 2024, https://www.aljazeera.com/news/2024/7/23/palestinian-rivals-hamas-and-fatah-sign-unity-deal-brokered-by-china.

in the vision. Nations are indeed coming into alignment to attack Israel.

2. In the second part of the vision, I saw nations planning to attack America during the time of the presidential election, getting closer to November 2024, capitalizing on the media frenzy that would surround former President Trump in the election. The plan was to attack America while she was in transition and vulnerable during the election season. Remember, God revealed this during our midnight prayer watch on January 27, 2024.

Six months after the vision, on July 13, 2024, a sniper tried to assassinate former president Donald Trump at a rally in Butler, Pennsylvania. No matter what your political party is, it's important to recognize that bloodshed of any kind is not good for any nation. If there is civil unrest on our soil, it will affect everyone, including our children and generations to come. Please also consider that the controversy over former President Trump is as much about him being pro-Israel as his personality. Anti-Israel nations would not benefit from America having a pro-Israel president.

Eleven days after the assassination attempt on July 24, 2024, Russia and China flew air bombers together for the first time in international airspace off the coast of Alaska. It was the first time Chinese bomber aircraft had flown within the Alaskan Air Defense

Identification Zone. More alarming, it was the first time Chinese and Russian aircraft had taken off from the same base in northeast Russia.[4] Nations are collaborating for an attack.

The vision and current events let us know what's happening is bigger than us. It's bigger than one person or political party. Our nation, and the world for that matter, have fundamentally shifted. Sixty nations have elections in 2024.[5] National leaders are shifting, setting the stage for accelerating end-time events.

This year, sixty nations have elections. The world will and has shifted, setting the stage for accelerating end-time events.

I have never seen America be so anti-Israel and anti-God, for that matter. I was not prepared for the propaganda and protesting that would take place in

---

[4] Lolita C. Baldor and Didi Tang, "Chinese and Russian bombers patrolling off Alaska raise concerns about growing military cooperation," July 26, 2024, accessed July 31, 2024, https://apnews.com/article/china-russia-us-military-planes-norad-alaska-4994b489e75ae636b4a4cd5bb40f91ac.

[5] Koh Ewe, "The Ultimate Election Year: All the Elections Around the World in 2024," Time Magazine, December 28, 2023, accessed August 3, 2024, https://time.com/6550920/world-elections-2024/.

response to Hamas' attack on Israel. Later, the Holy Spirit reminded me that Satan is the "prince of the power of the air" (Ephesians 2:2). He works through the airwaves of the media, using propaganda to *prop up his agenda*.

The anti-Israel protests are the enemy's "prop-agenda" to cloud people's minds and blind them to the wickedness at work behind the scenes. And the reality that being anti-Israel is being anti-God was nowhere in my mind when God was opening my spiritual eyes. He calls Himself the "God of Israel," and the Scriptures say, "Pray for the peace of Jerusalem: "May they prosper who love you" (Psalm 122:6 NKJV).

What I saw that night may or may not be the precipice of World War III, but it has become crystal clear that we need to pray against coordinated attacks on our nation and execute God's judgment against them and the agendas of nations who seek our nation's destruction. For this reason, and the things predicted in the Scripture, I know this is a season that God calls believers to watch for America and the nations fervently. So, writing this book is part of my responsibility to sound an alarm.

> *I know this is a season that God calls*
> *believers to watch for America and the*
> *nations fervently. So, writing this book*
> *is part of my responsibility to sound an*
> *alarm.*

We must watch and pray like never before; slumber leads to destruction.

In Matthew 24 and Luke 21, Jesus explains end-time events that will precede His return. He said, "Watch therefore, and pray always that you may be counted worthy to escape all these things that will come to pass, and to stand before the Son of Man" (Luke 21:36 NKJV). He spoke of His return coming like a snare upon all on Earth. So, as the Day of the Lord approaches, we must discipline ourselves to watch and pray even more. We must be alert, anticipating His return. This is the impetus for New Testament watching—the Lord's return and the events that will precede it.

"Be always on the watch, and pray that you may be able to escape all that is about to happen, and that you may be able to stand before the Son of Man." – Jesus in Luke 21:36 NIV)

Still, I see a state of slumber and laziness in the Church. Many believers rely on their pastor or priest to pray for them. Many who do pray only pray for themselves and their children. Many more have no idea of the agendas behind the scenes to pass evil laws and acts that will disfavor their faith and the future of their children and nation(s). They are not decreeing, declaring, and legislating God's Kingdom in prayer. No, they are sleeping, and "while men slept, his enemy came and sowed tares among the wheat and went his way" (Matthew 13:25 KJV). Because of spiritual slumber, much of the Church has not even recognized that the enemy has been sowing wrong seeds in their backyard. They are not connecting Scripture with what's happening in the world and with Israel right now.

Watching is not for a select few.

This is why relegating our duty to watch and pray to an anointed, select few is so dangerous. Indeed, some, like Prophet Anna, are graced to remain in fasting and prayer day and night (Luke 2:37). However, watching and praying is not for a select few anointed folks chosen by God to somehow miraculously stay awake while others sleep.

No, watching in prayer is a deliberate sacrifice resulting from a revelation of the urgency of the times. It is the duty of every New Testament believer.

9

> *Watching in prayer is a deliberate*
> *sacrifice resulting from a revelation of*
> *the urgency of the times.*

However, because we have called it an "anointing," many lazy believers have exempted themselves from their New Testament responsibility. Thus, they are falling asleep and in a state of spiritual stupor.

Paul said, "Besides all this, you know at what point of history we stand; so it is high time for you to rouse yourselves from sleep; for the final deliverance is nearer than when we first came to trust" (Romans 13:11 CJB). Rousing yourself means it's an individual responsibility to take action to do it; it's not a supernatural force coming on you, forcing you to do it. No, you rouse yourself; you take the action.

> *". . . you know at what point of history we stand; so it is high time for you to rouse yourselves from sleep; for the final deliverance is nearer than when we first came to trust." – Paul in Romans 13:11 CJB*

I am not saying the term "watchman anointing" is not legitimate. No, I am saying we each have a responsibility to watch and pray; it is not only the responsibility of prophets but all believers. In light of what God revealed to me on January 27, 2024, and what He is revealing to so many others, we need to watch and pray even more with a solid understanding of what the Bible means when it says to watch and pray.

So, I sound an alarm and shout that watching and praying is not the privilege of a few select anointed ones but the responsibility of every New Testament believer.

So, I sound an alarm and shout that watching and praying is not the privilege of a few select anointed ones but the responsibility of every New Testament believer.

The nations need watchers like never before. Will you awaken (or re-awaken) to our shared responsibility?

Recap and Reflect

In this chapter, we explored the vision from January 27, 2024, and the associated current events that corroborate its validity and illuminate our heightened need to watch and pray. We were reminded that what's happening is bigger than us! Our nation, and the world for that matter, have fundamentally shifted, setting the stage for accelerating end-time events. We must fight the spirit of slumber and watch and pray like never before.

Believers must pause and ensure that an understanding of the Scriptures and end-time events shape their worldview, who they vote for, and how they pray. God wants to execute judgement but wants to use believers who have understanding to do so. "To execute on them the written judgment—This honor have all His saints. Praise the Lord!" (Psalm 149:9 NKJV).

To aid our foundation and understanding, in the next chapter, we explore Old Testament watchmen and the insights they give us into our New Testament responsibility to watch and pray. In subsequent chapters, we explore Jesus' instructions on watching and praying, the watcher's process, the need to watch and pray for our nation(s), and crucial Scriptural reasons why we must watch and pray. Let's continue.

CHAPTER 2: OLD TESTAMENT WATCHMEN

"For thus hath the Lord said unto me, Go, set a watchman, let him declare what he seeth." – Prophet Isaiah in Isaiah 21:6 KJV

Old Testament watchmen often guarded vineyards, crops, and flocks. In an agricultural culture, people grew their own food and raised their own flocks. Without successful crops and flocks, their daily survival was at stake. So, watchers stood guard on the lookout for predators, thieves, and anything or anyone else that threatened the vitality of their crops and flocks. Shepherds watched over their sheep by night, and watchers climbed the watchtower, a tower for lookout,[6] to watch over crops and vineyards. Note the following Scriptures as examples:

> . . . My loved one *had a vineyard on a fertile hillside.* [2] He dug it up and cleared it of stones and planted it with the choicest vines. *He built a watchtower in it* and cut out a winepress as well. . . (Isaiah 5:1-2 NIV, italics added)

---

[6] Merriam-Webster.com Dictionary, s.v. "watchtower," accessed August 6, 2024, https://www.merriam-webster.com/dictionary/watchtower.

> *He also built towers* in the wilderness and dug
> many cisterns, *because he had much livestock* in
> the foothills and in the plain. He had people
> working his fields and vineyards in the hills
> and in the fertile lands, for he loved the soil. (2
> Chronicles 26:10 NIV, italics added)

These Scriptures show that watchtowers were built in
vineyards and in the foothills where livestock were
kept. Watchers stayed awake to climb the tower, look
out, and alert owners of pending predators and
destruction so they did not destroy the harvest
(increase). This is one of the first lessons we learn from
Old Testament watchers.

Watchers are vitally important for harvests.

For example, Gideon threshed wheat in a winepress
to hide from Midianites who would steal the harvest
(Judges 6:11).

> Whenever the Israelites planted their crops,
> the Midianites, Amalekites and other eastern
> peoples invaded the country. ⁴They camped
> on the land and ruined the crops all the way to
> Gaza and did not spare a living thing for
> Israel, neither sheep nor cattle nor
> donkeys. ⁵They came up with their livestock
> and their tents like swarms of locusts. It was
> impossible to count them or their camels; they

14

invaded the land to ravage it. [6] Midian so impoverished the Israelites that they cried out to the LORD for help. [11] The angel of the LORD came and sat down under the oak in Ophrah that belonged to Joash the Abiezrite, where his son Gideon was threshing wheat in a winepress to keep it from the Midianites. (Judges 6:3-6, 11 NIV)

It is essential to increase our watching and praying during harvest times.

Physically, that is when predators come to steal the results of planting, cultivating, and labor. Spiritually, there is a great end-time harvest of souls ready to be reaped. Like physical predators, the enemy comes to snatch people's understanding after the seed of the Word is planted—a seed that should be cultivated to reap conviction and repentance in their hearts—the harvest of soul salvation. Matthew 13:19 says, "When anyone hears the message about the kingdom and does not understand it, the evil one comes and snatches away what was sown in their heart. This is the seed sown along the path" (NIV).

There is a battle over the message of the Kingdom, and over the Kingdom itself. Nations are rallying, and no less than sixty nations have elections in 2024.[7] Like chess pieces, the enemy attempts to move kings and queens to set the stage for a one-world, one-government order (Revelation 13:3-17). God watches over His Word to perform it, and we need to watch and pray over the message of the Kingdom to ensure it advances. "Then the LORD said to me, "You have seen well, for I am [actively] watching over My word to fulfill it" (Jeremiah 1:12 AMP).

So many times, I have seen faith in some to receive the preached Word of God while the enemy distracted the minds of others. Few realize that a battle is going on while seated to receive the Word. Few come to Church vigilant and determined to stay alert and hear what the Spirit of the Lord will say. Some physically fall asleep during services, reflecting their spiritual state.

Few watch and pray as they listen, so the Word of God never penetrates. It never becomes engrafted or implanted. Thus, there is no transformation. ". . . Receive with meekness the implanted word, which is able to save your souls" (James 1:21 NKJV). An implanted word is one that takes root in the heart as a seed successfully planted in the ground that grows and bears fruit.

---

[7] Koh Ewe, "The Ultimate Election Year: All the Elections Around the World in 2024," Time Magazine, December 28, 2023, accessed August 3, 2024, https://time.com/6550920/world-elections-2024/.

There is a great end-time harvest of souls awaiting, but if we don't watch and pray, the Word will not take root, grow, and bear fruit. That kind of Word can bring salvation and transformation—the one that takes root. If the enemy snatches the Word, the harvest of salvation will not manifest. We must increase our watching and praying during harvest times. Watchwomen and men (watchers) are vital to harvests.

Old Testament watchers watched over their city, walking its walls.

In the ancient world, a city was a group of homes surrounded by a wall.[8] Without the wall, homes were vulnerable and unprotected from invasion. Walls of larger cities, like the broad wall referenced in Nehemiah 3:8, could measure 22 ft. wide, 25 ft. high, and two and a half miles long.[9] Towers were built atop these walls for watchers to lookout and guard the city. Note the following Scripture as an example:

> "The watchmen found me *as they made their rounds in the city*. They beat me, they bruised me; they

---

[8] Bible Project, "The Significance of the City in the Bible," YouTube Video, 7:01, July 24, 2023,
https://youtu.be/5yZLFmVHfaw?si=bhu9UGTsFfthDC92.

[9] City of David, "The Broad Wall (Episode 27) – City of David: Bringing the Bible to Life," YouTube Video, 2:15, June 15, 2022, https://youtu.be/9vAGOYRDk9w?si=7642BX0wAk5rC7PP.

took away my cloak, those *watchmen of the walls*!" (Song of Solomon 5:7 NIV, italics added).

The watchers walked the city walls, making rounds at night to detect and evict intruders by force. While everyone else slept, watchers ensured others could sleep in peace. They sacrificed slumber to deal with nighttime intruders.

Oh, how New Testament believers must do the same! They must serve as watchers in prayer, walking back and forth in late night, early morning, and noon prayer, sacrificing slumber to evict, rebuke, and bind spiritual intruders and the terror by night (Psalm 91:5).

We need men who will walk the floors of their bedrooms at night, calling on the name of the Lord for our nation's protection. We need women who will walk the floors of their children's bedrooms, anointing them with oil while they sleep and claiming their precious souls for Jesus. We need men and women who will walk the halls and streets of their state capitols, decreeing and declaring the Word of the Lord over the legislature, overturning evil laws and acts, and more.

Where are you, watchmen and women? The kingdom needs you like never before. Are you a mother who can only pray at night after putting the children to bed? Are you a father who rises early?

No matter your situation, the Kingdom needs watchers day and night.

> "I have posted watchmen on your walls, Jerusalem; they will never be silent day or night. You who call on the Lord, give yourselves no rest" (Isaiah 62:6 NIV).

Isaiah 62:6, an Old Testament scripture, helps us understand New Testament realities, namely:

1. Old Testament (OT) watchers were posted. As a New Testament (NT) watcher, you are posted on assignment.
2. OT watchers were posted on the city's wall, a high or elevated place. NT believers must stay in the high place of prayer.
3. OT watchers were not silent day or night. NT believers must watch and pray day and night for our cities and nations in shifts.
4. OT watchers did not give themselves any rest. Being a New Testament watcher is as much about discipline and availability as anything else. Anointed watchers who are undisciplined will be ineffective. What good is an anointing if you are fast asleep snoring with it?

5. OT watchers were posted to a geographic region. The NT watcher is responsible to watch and pray for their city, state, and nation.

Being a New Testament watcher is as much about discipline and availability as anything else. Anointed watchers who are undisciplined will be ineffective. What good is an anointing if you are fast asleep snoring with it?

It's important to remember that the peace of the country you live in affects your peace. For example, riots and civil conflict affect innocent bystanders, including children, and the COVID-19 pandemic did not discriminate in the way that so many plagued by ignorance do. We are all impacted in one way or another by what happens in our cities and nations. Thus, we have practical examples of the reality of Jeremiah 29:7, which says, "Also, do good things for the city I sent you to. Pray to the Lord for the city you are living in, because if there is peace in that city, you will have peace also" (ERV).

While America is not perfect, and no country is, as believers, we do have an obligation to pray for her like never before, especially considering our pending elections and recent events. We are called to watch for our cities, states, and nations.

Old Testament prophets watched over and warned people.

God spoke to His people Israel through Prophet Jeremiah, saying, "Also *I set watchmen over you*, saying, Hearken to the sound of the trumpet. But they said, We will not hearken" (Jeremiah 6:17 KJV, italics added). God set watchers over His people to warn them, but they would not listen.

Today, we are also called to watch for people: our families, communities, leaders, fellow believers, and all men. Paul put it this way, "I urge, then, first of all, that petitions, prayers, intercession, and thanksgiving be made for all people—for kings and all those in authority, that we may live peaceful and quiet lives in all godliness and holiness" (1 Timothy 2:1-2 NIV). In Colossians, he says, "Continue in prayer, and watch in the same with thanksgiving" (Colossians 4:2 KJV). Paul gives this imperative to all believers, not a select or an exclusive group of anointed ones. God calls us all to watch over others in prayer.

The church woke up to this imperative after Herod assassinated Apostle James and intended to do the same to Apostle Peter:

> And he killed James the brother of John with the sword. ³ And because he saw it pleased the Jews, he proceeded further to take Peter also. (Then were the days of unleavened bread.) ⁴ And when he had apprehended him, he put him in prison, and delivered him to four quaternions of soldiers to keep him; intending after Easter to bring him forth to the people. ⁵ Peter therefore was kept in prison: *but prayer was made without ceasing of the church unto God for him.* (Acts 12:2-5 KJV, italics added)

Herod wanted to kill Peter, *"but prayer was made without ceasing of the church unto God for him."* The enemy's plans were averted because the Church sacrificed sleep, watched, and prayed continuously for Peter. We need to watch and pray for our families, children, communities, leaders, fellow believers, and all men to avert the wicked plans of the evil one.

Recap and Reflect

In this chapter, we have gleaned insights from the Old Testament into our New Testament responsibility to watch and pray. Old Testament watchers were on the lookout for predators, thieves, and anything or anyone that threatened harvests, city walls, and the people in their city. It is vital that we increase our watching during harvest times, as there is a great end-time harvest of souls underway. Isaiah 62:6 also gives us no less than five solid insights into our watcher-responsibility.

Consider that God has assigned you—posted you—to watch and pray. Are you praying for your city, state, and nation? He said, "Also, do good things for the city I sent you to. Pray to the Lord for the city you are living in, because if there is peace in that city, you will have peace also" (ERV).

In the next chapter, we explore another key insight from the Old Testament—the watcher's process. We specify how to watch in the Spirit, detail the process, and define the word "watchman" to further clarify our role.

CHAPTER 3: THE WATCHER'S PROCESS

"Human being, I have appointed you to be a watchman for the house of Isra'el. When you hear a word from my mouth, you are to warn them for me." – God in Ezekiel 3:17 CJB

Many believers are intimidated by the phrase "watch and pray" because they don't feel capable of seeing in the Spirit and are unsure how or what they should watch for. However, the primary challenge of being able to watch in the Spirit is consistently positioning yourself to look. If you don't climb the tower of prayer consistently, you won't be positioned to see anything. Moreover, there is a process revealed in Ezekiel 3:17 that every believer can follow to exercise ourselves in watching and praying.

The primary challenge of being able to watch in the Spirit is consistently positioning yourself to look. If you don't climb the tower of prayer consistently, you won't be positioned to see anything.

Let's explore Ezekiel 3:17 to define the word watchman and then detail the watcher's process. First, God says, "Son of man, I have made thee a watchman unto the house of Israel . . ." (KJV). Some interpret this to mean that Ezekiel was made a watchman because he was a prophet, and only prophets can be watchmen. But notice the Complete Jewish Bible version of this verse. It says, "Human being, I have appointed you to be a watchman for the house of Isra'el." And we know that God appointed other watchmen who were not prophets because He said, "I have posted watchmen on your walls, Jerusalem; they will never be silent day or night. You who call on the LORD, give yourselves no rest" (Isaiah 62:6 NIV). That means if you have the ability to call on the name of the Lord, you have the ability to be a watchman.

So, let's understand what the word means. In Ezekiel 3:17, the word watchman is the Hebrew word *tsa.phah (or sapa)*, and it means:

- to look out or about, observe, watch
- to keep watch, spy
- watch closely[10]

---

[10] "Lexicon :: Strong's H6822 – *sapa*", Blue Letter Bible Study Tools, accessed August 2, 2024, https://www.blueletterbible.org/lexicon/h6822/kjv/wlc/0-1/.

All aspects of the definition require staying awake, alert, and positioned to look. We do that by accepting our identity as watchers and disciplining ourselves to be positioned to look through prayer. After that, we can begin the watcher's process embedded in Ezekiel 3:17.

The Watcher's Process

I call the watcher's process "W.W.W.":

1. Watch (Get in position and look.)
2. Word (Hear or see the burden on God's heart.)
3. Warn (Sound the alarm.)

1. Watch (Get in position and look.)

Human being, I have appointed you to be a watchman for the house of Isra'el. . . (Ezekiel 3:17a CJB)

By definition, a watcher is a lookout, spy, or careful observer. This is the first part of the process. Do not slumber, but stay awake and sacrifice sleep to get in a prayer position and look. Note what the watcher did in the following verse:

> And David sat between the two gates: and *the watchman went up to the roof over the gate unto the wall, and lifted up his eyes, and looked,* and behold a man running alone. (2 Samuel 18:24 KJV, italics added)

He went up to get in position, lifted his eyes, and looked. As a result, he observed a man running. Sometimes watchers see (the sight of someone coming), and sometimes they hear (the noise of running).

We, too, must position ourselves in the place of prayer and look. This could mean waiting in silence, worshipping, or praying in the Spirit until we hear or see something. But as you begin, pray for your nation, those in authority, and all men. Then, ask the Lord to reveal something. Ask Him what's on His heart for your nation for you to pray about, and I assure you, you will not waste your time. The Scripture says one of the few things God seeks is someone to stand in the gap. So, if you position yourself and make yourself available, He will speak or show you something— even if it takes some time for you to tune to His frequency, expect Him to reveal something by His Spirit. This takes us to the next step in the process.

2. Word (Hear or see the burden on God's heart.)

". . . When you hear a word from my mouth . . ." — God in Ezekiel 3:17b CJB

Once you are positioned to look (see or hear), ask God to reveal the burden on His heart and expect an answer—expect a word from His mouth. Jesus said, ". . . the sheep follow him: for they know his voice. And a stranger will they not follow . . ." (John 10:4-5 KJV). Spiritual hearing and eyesight are promised to us in the Scripture.

Jesus said the Holy Spirit shows us things to come. This is part of what I call the Holy Spirit's job description. He gives us advanced knowledge by opening our spiritual eyes to see things before they happen. Please note the following Scripture:

> Howbeit when he, the Spirit of truth, is come, he will guide you into all truth: for he shall not speak of himself; but whatsoever he shall hear, *that shall he speak: and he will shew you things* to come. (John 16:13 KJV, italics added)

According to John 16:13, the Holy Spirit speaks *and* shows (words and pictures). We are in the era of the outpouring of the Spirit. The Holy Spirit has come and, therefore, is available to show us things to come. This is not only for prophets but also for every believer who will cultivate a relationship with the Holy Spirit.

So, the second step in the process, seeing or hearing the burden from God's mouth, is possible for every believer with the Holy Spirit's help. Trust God for the spiritual hearing and eyesight promised in the Scriptures. Remember, "The hearing ear, and the seeing eye, the Lord hath made even both of them" (Proverbs 20:12 KJV). Now, let's explore the third part of the process.

3. Warn (Sound the alarm.)

". . . you are to warn them for me." – God in Ezekiel 3:17c
CJB

The first patent for an electromagnetic burglar alarm was registered in 1853 by the Reverend Augustus Russell Pope of Somerville, Massachusetts.[11] In Bible times, there were no electronic doorbells or alarms. The watcher was the alarm system. Blood could be on his hands if he failed to sound the alarm.

Today, you are God's spiritual alarm system. He is counting on you to watch and pray to sound the alarm about what you see, sending warnings to avert crises. That is why I have been trying to tell everyone about what God showed me on January 27, 2024, and why I pray the words of this book will awaken and provoke others to watch and pray. Lives and nations are at stake.

Sound the alarm; you are the alarm signal. Submit what you see to your leaders, trusted advisors, and mentors. If you receive a warning for your family, tell

---

[11] "A HISTORY OF BURGLAR AN SECURITY ALARMS," Justice Security Company July 24, 2019, accessed August 1, 2024, https://www.justicesecurity.co.uk/blogs-item/a-history-of-burglar-and-security-alarms.

the head of the family. If you're the head of the family, share it with everyone else. If you receive a warning for your children, tell them. Sound the alarm in whatever way you can. Don't keep silent!

Remember:

1. Watch (Get in position and look.)
2. Word (Hear or see the burden on God's heart.)
3. Warn (Sound the alarm.)

Recap and Reflect

In this chapter, we have defined the word watchman and detailed the watcher's process, "W.W.W.": watch, word, and warn, emphasizing that through a relationship with the Holy Spirit, every believer can see, hear, and warn.

Reflect on John 16:13. It's part of the Holy Spirit's job description to show you things to come.

In the next chapter, we explore the New Testament Scriptures related to watching and praying, including Jesus' assessment of the matter and the need to fight the spirit of slumber attacking the Church.

CHAPTER 4: NEW TESTAMENT WATCHING: AGRYPNEO AND GREGOREO

"But of that day and hour no one knows, not even the angels in heaven, nor the Son, but only the Father. Take heed, watch and pray; for you do not know when the time is." – Jesus in Mark 13:32-33 NKJV

This chapter explores two New Testament words: agrypneo and gregoreo. As we explore these words and their associated Scriptures, we see Jesus' instructions on watching and praying and the need to resist the spirit of slumber that has gripped the church in America. Agrypneo is used four times in the KJV version, and gregoreo is used twenty-four times. Agrypneo is the Greek word for watching and being alert, used in Ephesians 6:18, listed below:

> Praying always with all prayer and supplication in the Spirit, and *watching* there unto with all perseverance and supplication for all saints. (Ephesians 6:18 KJV, italics added)

> And pray in the Spirit on all occasions with all kinds of prayers and requests. With this in mind, *be alert* and always keep on praying for

all the Lord's people. (Ephesians 6:18 NIV,
italics added)

Agrypneo means to:

- keep awake, keep alert

- be awake, watch

- be watchful, vigilant

- lie awake, pass sleepless nights[12]

Thus, in Ephesians 6:18, Paul tells us to pass sleepless nights praying in the Spirit in a state of alertness—with vigilance on all occasions, with all kinds of prayers and requests for all the Lord's people. This is an imperative he gives to all New Testament believers, and it does not align with the lackadaisical attitude I often see in the Church towards prayer. Instead, Paul paints a picture of a vigilant, disciplined people who take a serious approach to watching and praying to the extent they pass sleepless nights praying in tongues.

Again, being a New Testament watcher is as much about discipline and availability as anything else. Anointed watchers who are undisciplined will be ineffective. What good is an anointing if you are fast

---

[12] "Lexicon :: Strong's G69 – *agrypneō*", Blue Letter Bible Study Tools, accessed August 2, 2024,
https://www.blueletterbible.org/lexicon/g69/kjv/tr/0-1/.

asleep snoring with it? No! Paul tells us to spend sleepless nights watching in the Spirit.

Paul tells us to pass sleepless nights praying in the Spirit in a state of alertness — with vigilance on all occasions, with all kinds of prayers and requests for all the Lord's people. This is an imperative he gives to all New Testament believers.

This word agrypneo occurs in the following KJV Scriptures: Ephesians 6:18, which we already discussed, and Mark 13:33, Luke 21:36, and Hebrews 13:17, listed below.

Take heed, *watch and pray*; for you do not know when the time is. (Mark 13:33 KJV, italics added)

Be on guard! *Be alert!* You do not know when that time will come. (Mark 13:33 NIV, italics added)

In the passage in Mark 13, Jesus is speaking to his disciples about the events that will mark the end of the age and His return. He tells them—and us—to agrypneo: watch, be alert, and pass sleepless nights because we don't know the day of His return. Note that the KJV translates agrypneo as "watch," and the

NIV translates it as "be alert." The KJV and NIV versions are listed for the following "agrypneo" Scripture(s).

But take heed to yourselves, lest your hearts be weighed down with carousing, drunkenness, and cares of this life, and that Day come on you unexpectedly. ³⁵ For it will come as a snare on all those who dwell on the face of the whole earth. *³⁶ Watch therefore, and pray always that you may be counted worthy to escape all these things* that will come to pass, and to stand before the Son of Man. (Luke 21:36 KJV, italics added)

Be careful, or your hearts will be weighed down with carousing, drunkenness and the anxieties of life, and that day will close on you suddenly like a trap. ³⁵ For it will come on all those who live on the face of the whole earth. *³⁶ Be always on the watch, and pray that you may be able to escape all that is about to happen*, and that you may be able to stand before the Son of Man. (Luke 21:36 NIV, italics added)

Jesus is again speaking to us about the events that will mark the end of the age and His return. This time, He tells them—and us—to agrypneo: watch, be alert, and pass sleepless nights so that we'll be counted worthy to escape all that will happen. This is a message to all New Testament believers; we must live like we believe Jesus is coming back—because He is! And if we truly believe He is coming back, we will make watching and praying for His return a lifestyle.

Sound the alarm! Watch over the harvest (of souls) because we must work while it is day. The night comes when no man will work any longer (John 9:4).

The fourth Scripture that uses the word agrypneo is Hebrews 13:17:

> Have confidence in your leaders and submit to their authority, because they *keep watch* over you as those who must give an account. Do this so that their work will be a joy, not a burden, for that would be of no benefit to you. (Hebrews 13:17 NIV, italics added)

Spiritual leaders are supposed to agrypneo—watch over their members. Remember, Old Testament shepherds watched over their flocks at night, staying awake while the sheep slept. This is an awesome responsibility that, shockingly, is often overlooked. Many pastors focus only on the public pulpit to the neglect of their private prayer lives.

How many pastors (senior church leaders) do you know that can pray for an hour straight without reverting to preaching? Watch for an hour? Pray in the Spirit for an hour? Spend an hour praying for their members? Selah.

The second New Testament word for "watching" we explore is grēgoreō.

Gregoreo means to:

- keep watch; be on guard

- be awake, watch

- be alive, vigilant, active

- be watchful, attentive, circumspect or cautious, on guard, vigilant, and give strict attention to

- be roused from sleep

- become fully awake[13]

The word gregoreo is used twenty-four times in the KJV in the following thirteen Scriptures. Please read each of the following Scriptures and note the associated reasons and dynamics of watching and praying:

> **Watch** and pray, that ye enter not into temptation: the spirit indeed is willing, but the flesh is weak. (Matthew 26:41 KJV, emphasis added)

---

[13] "Lexicon :: Strong's G1127 – *grēgoreō*," Blue Letter Bible Study Tools, accessed August 2, 2024,
https://www.blueletterbible.org/lexicon/g1127/kjv/tr/0-1/.

> Watch and pray so that you will not fall into temptation. The spirit is willing, but the flesh is weak. (Matthew 26:41 NIV)

Matthew 26:41 reveals that our flesh is an enemy to our watching. We must overcome the flesh to watch, to become fully awake—that means we must be disciplined.

> **Watch** therefore: for ye know not what hour your Lord doth come. [43] But know this, that if the goodman of the house had known in what **watch** the thief would come, he would have **watched**, and would not have suffered his house to be broken up. (Matthew 24:42-43 KJV, emphasis added)

According to Matthew 24:42, one of the main reasons New Testament believers should watch and pray is in anticipation of the Lord's return and the events surrounding His return. Gregoreo means we should give full attention to His return, become fully awake to it, and be on guard for it.

> **Watch** therefore, for ye know neither the day nor the hour wherein the Son of man cometh. (Matthew 25:13 KJV, emphasis added)

> For the Son of Man is as a man taking a far journey, who left his house, and gave authority to his servants, and to every man his work, and

39

commanded the porter to **watch**. [35] **Watch** ye therefore: for ye know not when the master of the house cometh, at even, or at midnight, or at the cockcrowing, or in the morning: [36] Lest coming suddenly he find you sleeping. [37] And what I say unto you I say unto all, **Watch**. (Mark 13:34-37 KJV, emphasis added)

These Scriptures clarify that slumber is an enemy to vigilant, active watching. Jesus has given us authority and expects us to occupy until He returns.

And saith unto them, My soul is exceeding sorrowful unto death: tarry ye here, and **watch**. [35] And he went forward a little, and fell on the ground, and prayed that, if it were possible, the hour might pass from him. [36] And he said, Abba, Father, all things are possible unto thee; take away this cup from me: nevertheless not what I will, but what thou wilt. [37] And he cometh, and findeth them sleeping, and saith unto Peter, Simon, sleepest thou? couldest not thou **watch** one hour? [38] **Watch ye and pray**, lest ye enter into temptation. The spirit truly is ready, but the flesh is weak. (Mark 14:34-38 KJV, emphasis added)

In Mark 14, Jesus found His disciples sleeping. Slumber is an enemy of watching and praying. We must steadfastly resist the spirit of slumber and stupor that wants to keep the Church blind to what is happening behind the scenes in the realm of the Spirit. Jesus expected the disciples to be able to watch for at least an hour. Watching and praying helps us avoid temptation. Your reborn spirit will be willing to watch and pray, but your flesh will fight that willingness. Subdue the flesh to watch and pray.

> Blessed are those servants, whom the lord when he cometh shall find **watching**: verily I say unto you, that he shall gird himself, and make them to sit down to meat, and will come forth and serve them. (Luke 12:37 KJV, emphasis added)

There is a reward for those who will not slumber but be found watching when Jesus returns. According to Luke 12:37, He will serve them. While some are indeed prophets, the basis for the New Testament believer's watching is not whether they are prophets but anticipation of the Lord's return. Much of the Old Testament prophesied Jesus' birth—His coming. Now, we must herald His return. "In the past God spoke to our ancestors through the prophets at many times and in various ways, 2 but in these last days he has spoken to us by his Son, whom he appointed heir of all things, and through whom also he made the universe" (Hebrews 1:1-2 NIV).

> Therefore **watch**, and remember, that by the space of three years I **ceased not to warn** every one night

41

and day with tears. (Acts 20:31 KJV, emphasis added)

In Acts 20:31, Paul tells his followers, who were church leaders, to take heed to the flock because after he left them, grievous wolves would attack the flock (church members). He admonishes them to watch and pray and reminds them that he warned them day and night for three years. Yes, three years. Being a watcher is not for the fainthearted or undisciplined. Many nights, I have led midnight prayer while fighting the weight of physical sleepiness and fatigue. My eyelids were closing, but my tongues (praying in the Spirit) were still rolling! Thank God the same Spirit that raised Jesus from the dead quickens our mortal bodies and helps our infirmities when we pray (Romans 8:11, 26).

Watch, **stand** fast in the faith, **be brave, be strong**. (1 Corinthians 16:13 NKJV, emphasis added)

Continue in prayer, and **watch** in the same with thanksgiving. (Colossians 4:2 KJV, emphasis added)

Stand, be brave, be strong, continue! These are all military terms that align with the aspect of gregoreo that means to be vigilant.

Therefore let us not sleep, as do others; but let us **watch** and **be sober**. [7] For they that sleep sleep in the night; and they that be drunken are drunken in the night. [8] But let us, who are of the day, **be sober,** putting on the breastplate of faith and love; and for an helmet, the hope of salvation. [9] For God hath not appointed us to wrath, but to obtain salvation by our Lord Jesus Christ, [10] Who died for us, that, whether we wake or sleep, we should live together with him. (1 Thessalonians 5:6-10 KJV, emphasis added)

Be sober, **be vigilant**; because your adversary the devil, as a roaring lion, walketh about, seeking whom he may devour. (1 Peter 5:8 KJV, emphasis added)

Note from the previous verses that the antithesis of watching is sleeping. We must be sober. We must be vigilant. We cannot be people who love oversleeping.

Be **watchful**, and strengthen the things which remain, that are ready to die: for I have not found thy works perfect before God. [3] Remember therefore how thou hast received and heard, and hold fast, and repent. If therefore thou shalt not **watch**, I will come on thee as a thief, and thou shalt not know what hour I will come upon thee. (Revelation 3:2-3 KJV, emphasis added)

Behold, I come as a thief. Blessed is he that **watcheth**, and keepeth his garments, lest he walk naked, and they see his shame. (Revelation 16:15 KJV, emphasis added)

Watching will keep us in readiness for the Lord's return and help us to avoid shame on the Day of Judgment.

The basis for every New Testament believer's watching is not whether they are a prophet but anticipation of the Lord's return.

We must resist the spirit of slumber.

Physically, when someone is sleepy and drowsy, their eyes are heavy, making it difficult to see and hear clearly. When someone is fully asleep, their eyes are completely closed; they are blind to what's happening around them and cannot hear anything—even though there is still activity. We must avoid spiritually being in this state of drowsiness or slumber. Physical and spiritual sleep and slumber are enemies of watching and praying. That is why when the enemy attacks your prayer life, you must fight with everything in you to stand on your watch, and having done all to stand, stand some more. Take note of the dangers of not watching:

Remember therefore how thou hast received and heard, and hold fast, and repent. If therefore thou shalt not watch, I will come on thee as a thief, and thou shalt not know what hour I will come upon thee. (Revelation 3:3 KJV)

Watching is essential to preparedness for the Lord's return. Can you watch with Him for an hour?

Recap and Reflect

In this chapter, we explored seventeen Scriptures related to New Testament watching that establish watching and praying as every believer's responsibility because of the Lord's coming return.

What would you do differently if you knew Jesus was returning next year? Would your prayer life change? What if you knew an enemy planned to attack your child's school or city next month? Would you warn anyone?

In the next chapter, we explore our watcher responsibility in greater detail and in connection with our dominion mandate.

CHAPTER 5: OUR WATCHER RESPONSIBILITY: WE ARE IN CHARGE!

"When placed in command, take charge." – Norman Schwarzkopf

When God created us, He gave us a mandate. The first imperative He gave to mankind was not to praise or worship Him but to dominate—to be in charge.

> Then God said, "Let Us make man in Our image, according to Our likeness; let them have dominion over the fish of the sea, over the birds of the air, and over the cattle, over all the earth and over every creeping thing that creeps on the earth." [27] So God created man in His *own* image; in the image of God He created him; *male and female He created them.* [28] *Then God blessed them, and God said to them,* "Be fruitful and multiply; *fill the earth and subdue it;* have dominion over the fish of the sea, over the birds of the air, and over every living thing that moves on the earth." (Genesis 1:26-28 NKJV, italics added)

We have the same mandate today.

God blessed male and female and told them both to subdue the earth—to have dominion over it. God put male and female—mankind—in charge of Earth to extend His sovereign rule and Kingdom's domain from heaven to Earth. That is why Jesus instructed us to pray, "Thy Kingdom come, thy will be done on Earth, as it is in heaven" (Luke 11:2). That means we are in charge.

The passage in Psalm 8 makes that even clearer, calling us a little lower than God and in charge. Read carefully:

> What are mere mortals that you should think about them, human beings that you should care for them? [5] Yet you made them only a little lower than God and crowned them with glory and honor. [6] You gave them charge of everything you made, putting all things under their authority. (Psalm 8:4-6 NLT)

If, as Psalm 8:5 says, God put us in charge and gave us authority over all things, we can't blame Him when bad things happen because we are not watching and praying, standing on guard to protect that which is under our charge. We have so much authority that He told us whatever we stand in agreement and allow will be allowed, and whatever we stand in agreement and disallow on Earth will be disallowed. Consider the following version of that familiar passage:

48

Yes! I tell you people that *whatever you prohibit on earth will be prohibited in heaven, and whatever you permit on earth will be permitted in heaven.* [19] To repeat, I tell you that if two of you here on earth agree about anything people ask, it will be for them from my Father in heaven. (Matthew 18:18-19 CJB, italics added)

Again, this Scripture tells us that Earth is our domain, and we bring the influence of heaven into it via prayer. We are the watchers, protectors, and guardians of the domain called Earth. It is our responsibility to watch for our families, communities, cities, and nations. We are in charge! According to Psalm 115, the earth is our domain:

"The highest heavens belong to the Lord, but the earth he has given to mankind." — Unnamed Psalmist in Psalm 115:16 NIV

"The heaven, even the heavens, are the Lord's; But the earth He has given to the children of men." — Unnamed Psalmist in Psalm 115:16 NKJV

Jesus ascended like a man who had taken a trip to a faraway land. He left us in charge of Earth, telling us to occupy until He returns (Luke 19:13). We are responsible for legislating, binding, loosing, decreeing, declaring, watching, and praying concerning what happens on Earth. We bring God into Earth's affairs through partnership in prayer.

The Earth is our domain, which means we are responsible for legislating, binding, loosing, decreeing, declaring, watching, and praying concerning what happens on Earth. We bring God into Earth's affairs through partnership in prayer.

If we take an honest assessment, we may find that some negative things in our lives result from a lack of vigilance in prayer. The enemy may have planted some things while we were sleeping and not watching and praying. "But while men slept, his enemy came and sowed tares among the wheat, and went his way" (Matthew 13:25 KJV). The enemy may have sown wrong friends into our children's lives or wrong ideas through social media because we were too tired from work to be vigilant in prayer or check on what they were doing. The enemy may have sown wrong laws, bills, and acts through our nation's congress because we were too busy to watch and pray or even be concerned or write our district and state representatives to remind them that they still have Bible-believing constituents.

Earth is our domain; we are in charge; therefore, we must be her guardians and watchers.

> *Earth is our domain; we are in charge;*
> *therefore, we must be her guardians*
> *and watchers.*

We are watchers individually and corporately as the Church. God intended to use us, His Church, to speak to principalities and legislate His Kingdom's rulership, laws, and principles on Earth. According to the Apostle Paul, this is part of God's eternal purpose. Paul said:

> To me, who am less than the least of all the saints, this grace was given, that I should preach among the Gentiles the unsearchable riches of Christ, [9] and to make all see what *is* the fellowship of the mystery, which from the beginning of the ages has been hidden in God who created all things through Jesus Christ; [10] *to the intent that now the manifold wisdom of God might be made known by the church to the principalities and power*s in the heavenly *places*, [11] *according to the eternal purpose* which He accomplished in Christ Jesus

51

our Lord. (Ephesians 3:8-11 NKJV, italics added)

Please note verse ten: "To the intent that now the manifold wisdom of God might be made known by the church to the principalities and powers in the heavenly places." Part of our responsibility as the Church is to declare the wisdom of God to principalities and powers to veto anything they decree or plan that is in opposition to the counsel of God. Watching and praying empowers us to do that.

Recap and Reflect

This chapter briefly explored our dominion mandate and the reality that God has put us in charge of Earth. He gave us the authority to permit, allow, veto, or disallow what happens on Earth. Our responsibility is to be on the lookout and guard our families, children, communities, churches, cities, and nations. As the people in charge, we bring God into Earth's affairs through partnership in prayer.

In the next chapter, we explore the role of God's holy angels in watching and praying, specifically over nations. We examine what Daniel meant by the phrase "the decree of the watchers."

CHAPTER 6: THE DECREE OF THE WATCHERS: NATIONS AT STAKE

"This matter is by the decree of the watchers, and the demand by the word of the holy ones: to the intent that the living may know that the most High ruleth in the kingdom of men, and giveth it to whomsoever he will, and setteth up over it the basest of men." — The Watcher who visited King Nebuchadnezzar

Nebuchadnezzar had a dream in which someone he identified as a "watcher" announced a verdict, a decree, concerning his kingship and nation. But the watcher wasn't a human being. Nebuchadnezzar describes his dream in the book of Daniel:

I, Nebuchadnezzar, was at home in my palace, contented and prosperous. ⁵I had a dream that made me afraid. As I was lying in bed, the images and visions that passed through my mind terrified me. ⁶So I commanded that all the wise men of Babylon be brought before me to interpret the dream for me. ⁷When the magicians, enchanters, astrologers and diviners came, I told them the dream, but they could not interpret it for me. [8] Finally, Daniel came into my presence and I told him the dream. (He is called Belteshazzar, after the name of my god, and the spirit of the holy gods is in him.) [9] I said, "Belteshazzar, chief of the magicians, I know that the spirit of the holy gods is in you, and no mystery is too difficult for you. Here is my dream; interpret it for me. [10] These are the visions I saw while lying in bed: I looked, and there before me stood a tree in the middle of the land. Its height was enormous. [11] The tree grew large and strong and its top touched the sky; it was visible to the ends of the earth. [12] Its leaves were beautiful, its fruit abundant, and on it was food for all. Under it the wild animals found shelter, and the birds lived in its branches; from it every creature was fed. [13] *"In the visions I saw while lying in bed, I looked, and there before me was a holy one, a messenger, coming down from heaven.* [14] He called in a loud voice: 'Cut down the tree and trim off its branches; strip off its leaves and scatter its fruit. Let the animals flee from under it and the birds from its branches. [15] But let the stump and its roots, bound with iron and bronze, remain in the ground, in the grass of the field. "'Let him be drenched with the dew of heaven, and let him live with the animals among the plants of the earth. [16] Let his mind be changed from that of a man and let him be given the mind of an animal, till seven times pass by for him. [17]"'The decision is announced by messengers, the holy ones declare the verdict, *so that the living may know that the Most High is sovereign over all kingdoms on earth and gives them to anyone he wishes and sets over them the lowliest of people.'* (Daniel 4:4-17 NIV, italics added)

Holy Watchers

In verse thirteen, it is clear that the "watcher" is one of God's holy angels coming down from heaven. Nebuchadnezzar says, "I saw in the visions of my head upon my bed, and, behold, *a watcher and an holy one* came down from heaven" (Daniel 4:13 KJV, italics added). The NIV translates the word watcher as "messenger." It is the Hebrew word עִיר (ir), which means a watcher, wakeful one, waking, and angel. It only occurs three times in the Old Testament and all three times in the book of Daniel concerning decrees and determinations over a king and nation.

In verse 17, the watcher clarifies that the verdict is so Nebuchadnezzar would know that God is Most High, sovereign over all kingdoms on Earth, and gives them to anyone he wishes. God is concerned about nations and wants us to watch over nations to establish His sovereign rule (His Kingdom) because the destinies of nations are at stake.

The NIV Cultural Backgrounds Study Bible has this note concerning the Daniel 4 watchers:

> The Aramaic noun used here means "one who is awake, a watcher." The "Watchers" are widely attested in Jewish literature of Hellenistic and early Roman period. The best-known example is "The Book of Watchers" in 1 Enoch 1-36, where the term usually refers to fallen angels. However, even in 1 Enoch the term is used of the (good) archangels (1 Enoch 20:1). There is no evidence outside of Daniel of the word "watcher" being used in this specialized way of heavenly beings before the 3rd century BC, though Mesopotamian religion included the idea of a variety of protecting deities or angels.[14]

Daniel 4:13 reminds us that angels watch and issue God's decrees over nations. There have been several occasions during the midnight prayer watch when angels entered my room in response to prayer. Sometimes, they would hand me a sword. Other times, they would wait for a directive; other times,

---

[14] *NIV Cultural Backgrounds Bible,* eds. John H. Walton and Craig S. Keener (Grand Rapids, MI: Zondervan, 2016), 1,425.

they would show me the spoils of our victory in prayer.

Angels are deployed by our prayers. Remember, when Peter was in prison, angels executed his jailbreak in response to the Church's prayer (Acts 12:5). God's holy angels do the same today; they respond to the Church's prayer.

We must expect God's holy angels to respond to our prayers and decrees today.

Daniel's encounter reveals there may be a special category or rank of holy angels assigned to watch over nations. The devil mimics what he saw in heaven and has assigned his own evil, "prince-level" unholy angels called principalities over nations. One holy angel testified that the unholy angel, the "prince of Persia," withstood him. "But the prince of the Persian kingdom resisted me twenty-one days. Then Michael, one of the chief princes, came to help me because I was detained there with the king of Persia" (Daniel 10:13 NIV).

As we watch and pray over nations, we must deploy the ministry of God's holy angels (watchers). "Are not all angels ministering spirits sent to serve those who will inherit salvation?" (Hebrews 1:14 NIV).

> *The Hebrew word* עִיר *(ir) for*
> *watchers only occurs three times in the*
> *Old Testament and all three times in*
> *the book of Daniel chapter four*
> *concerning decrees and determinations*
> *over a king and nation. God is*
> *concerned about nations and wants to*
> *watch over nations because the*
> *destinies of nations are at stake.*

We must expect God's holy angels to work with our prayers because they do the bidding of His Word and are the military of our Heavenly Kingdom. Jehovah is the Lord of Hosts, the God of angel armies. As we watch and pray for our nation(s), we must be aware that holy angel watchers are watching with us. They are waiting for us to pronounce the Word of God and the decrees we hear from the mouth of God over nations so they can enforce them. Note the announcement in the following Scripture:

> *"'The decision is announced by messengers,* the holy ones declare the verdict, so that the living may know that the Most High is sovereign over all kingdoms on earth and gives them to anyone he wishes and sets over

them the lowliest of people.' (Daniel 4:17 NIV, italics added)

"This order is issued by the watchers, the sentence is announced by the holy ones, so that all who live may know that the Most High rules the human kingdom, that he gives it to whomever he wishes and can raise up over it the lowliest of mortals." (Daniel 4:17 CJB, italics added)

We must be aware that as we watch and pray for our nation, holy angel watchers are watching with us. They are waiting for us to pronounce the Word of God and the decrees we hear from the mouth of God over nations so they can enforce them.

God's holy angels will work with us to announce and enforce decrees as we legislate in the Spirit over our nations. We need the Lord to release them and work with us as we watch because "Unless the LORD builds the house, They labor in vain who build it; Unless the LORD guards the city, The watchman stays awake in vain" (Psalm 127:1 NKJV).

Nebuchadnezzar needed someone the Spirit of God could use to interpret the watcher's announcement for him. After Nebuchadnezzar explains his dream, Daniel interprets it. Here's what Daniel said in response to the watcher's announcement:

> "This is the dream that I, King Nebuchadnezzar, had. Now, Belteshazzar, tell me what it means, for none of the wise men in my kingdom can interpret it for me. But you can, because the spirit of the holy gods is in you." [19] Then Daniel (also called Belteshazzar) was greatly perplexed for a time, and his thoughts terrified him. So the king said, "Belteshazzar, do not let the dream or its meaning alarm you." Belteshazzar answered, "My lord, if only the dream applied to your enemies and its meaning to your adversaries! [20] The tree you saw, which grew large and strong, with its top touching the sky, visible to the whole earth, [21] with beautiful leaves and abundant fruit, providing food for all, giving shelter to the wild animals, and having nesting places in its branches for the birds— [22] Your Majesty, you are that tree! You have become great and strong; your greatness has grown until it reaches the sky, and your dominion extends to distant parts of the earth. [23] "Your Majesty saw a holy one, a messenger, coming down from heaven and saying, 'Cut down the tree and destroy it, but leave the stump, bound with iron and bronze, in the

grass of the field, while its roots remain in the ground. Let him be drenched with the dew of heaven; let him live with the wild animals, until seven times pass by for him.' ²⁴ *"This is the interpretation, Your Majesty, and this is the decree the Most High has issued against my lord the king:* ²⁵ *You will be driven away from people and will live with the wild animals; you will eat grass like the ox and be drenched with the dew of heaven. Seven times will pass by for you until you acknowledge that the Most High is sovereign over all kingdoms on earth and gives them to anyone he wishes.* (Daniel 4:18-25 NIV, italics added)

The kings of Earth (presidents, queens, heads of state, etc.) must acknowledge that the Most High is sovereign over all kingdoms on Earth and gives them to anyone he wishes.

Daniel's interpretation makes it clear that the issue was Nebuchadnezzar's lack of acknowledgment that God is the sovereign ruler over all kingdoms—not just the Kingdom of Heaven—but all kingdoms (nations) of Earth. God gives rulership of the nations to whomever He wishes.

If He has put us in charge through the dominion mandate, we must invite Him into the affairs of the Earth's nations through prayer. Esther fasted and prayed to overturn an evil law passed against her

61

people. Daniel's commitment to pray — in violation of an ungodly law — provoked the king to issue a proclamation that Daniel's God was the true God.

Like Daniel and Esther, we must invite God into the affairs of our nation(s) through fasting, watching, and praying. Nations are at stake. We must enforce God's rule, principles, and morality over the nations and their laws, values, and way of life as we pray, "Thy Kingdom come; thy will be done, on Earth as it is in heaven," as Jesus instructed.

After interpreting Nebuchadnezzar's dream, Daniel had his own vision. He saw the Ancient of Days seated in the court of heaven, giving the rule of all nations to Jesus.

> "In my vision at night I looked, and there before me was one like a son of man, coming with the clouds of heaven. He approached the Ancient of Days and was led into his presence. [14] He was given authority, glory and sovereign power; all nations and peoples of every language worshiped him. *His dominion is an everlasting dominion that will not pass away, and his kingdom is one that will never be destroyed.* [15] "I, Daniel, was troubled in spirit, and the visions that passed through my mind disturbed me. [16] I approached one of those standing there

and asked him the meaning of all this. "So he told me and gave me the interpretation of these things: [17] 'The four great beasts are four kings that will rise from the earth. [18] *But the holy people of the Most High will receive the kingdom and will possess it forever—yes, for ever and ever.'* [19] "Then I wanted to know the meaning of the fourth beast, which was different from all the others and most terrifying, with its iron teeth and bronze claws—the beast that crushed and devoured its victims and trampled underfoot whatever was left. [20] I also wanted to know about the ten horns on its head and about the other horn that came up, before which three of them fell—the horn that looked more imposing than the others and that had eyes and a mouth that spoke boastfully. [21] *As I watched, this horn was waging war against the holy people and defeating them,* [22] *until the Ancient of Days came and pronounced judgment in favor of the holy people of the Most High, and the time came when they possessed the kingdom.* [23] "He gave me this explanation: 'The fourth beast is a fourth kingdom that will appear on earth. It will be different from all the other kingdoms and will devour the whole earth, trampling it down and crushing it. [24] The ten horns are ten kings who will come from this kingdom. *After them another king will arise, different from the earlier*

> *ones; he will subdue three kings.* ²⁵*He will speak against the Most High and oppress his holy people and try to change the set times and the laws.* The holy people will be delivered into his hands for a time, times and half a time. ²⁶ *"'But the court will sit, and his power will be taken away and completely destroyed forever.* ²⁷*Then the sovereignty, power and greatness of all the kingdoms under heaven will be handed over to the holy people of the Most High. His kingdom will be an everlasting kingdom, and all rulers will worship and obey him.'* ²⁸ "This is the end of the matter. I, Daniel, was deeply troubled by my thoughts, and my face turned pale, but I kept the matter to myself." (Daniel 7:13-28 NIV, italics added)

Please note in verse twenty-one that the impetus behind the war that was raging was an anti-God and anti-God's holy people agenda. And remember, in my January 27th vision, anti-God nations were collaborating to attack Israel.

Times and laws are changing; nations are at stake.

Also, note in verse twenty-five that the king tried to change the times and laws. Today, the times and laws are changing. There are laws related to families, the gender identity of our children, and abortion that would have never been dreamed of two decades ago.

64

Will we ever know how many future apostles, prophets, evangelists, pastors, and teachers have been destroyed by abortions or gender-transforming drugs? We now have laws that institutionalize and allow the same wicked spirit of abortion that tried to assassinate Moses and our Messiah. Moreover, concerning the change of times, if we look at current world events in the light of Daniel's visions, specifically Daniel 7:24-25, we must know that a greater one-world, anti-God government agenda is at play (Revelation 13:3-17).

Daniel's vision doesn't mean we acquiesce to evil rule and rulers over nations as an inevitable reality. No, the Kingdom of Heaven must forcefully advance even while violent people try to hijack it. "And from the time John the Baptist began preaching until now, the Kingdom of Heaven has been forcefully advancing, and violent people are attacking it" (Matthew 11:12 NLT). Though the Kingdom and what it stands for is attacked by wicked laws, God told Abraham He would spare wicked Sodom and Gomorrah for the sake of fifty righteous. I dare say there are more than fifty righteous people in our nation.

We must rise, awaken out of slumber, watch, and pray for God's mercy to avert crisis, calamity, and the effects of pending war(s). We must enforce Jesus' Kingdom, praying and declaring, "Thy Kingdom come, thy will be done, on Earth, as it is in heaven.

65

According to Prophet Isaiah, ultimately, Jesus will rule the nations, His Kingdom will come down from heaven to Earth, and we will rule with him:

> Of the greatness of his government and peace there will be no end. He will reign on David's throne and over his kingdom, establishing and upholding it with justice and righteousness from that time on and forever. The zeal of the Lord Almighty will accomplish this. (Isaiah 9:7 NIV)

> "Also your people shall all be righteous; they shall inherit the land forever, the branch of My planting, the work of My hands, that I may be glorified." (Isaiah 60:21 NIV)

We must remember the victory promised in these Scriptures to boldly and courageously watch, pray, decree, declare, and legislate in these end-times and amid growing persecution. The righteous are as bold as a lion (Proverbs 28:1). Will you be bold to watch and pray and decree and declare?

Recap and Reflect

In this chapter, we discussed the identity of the watchers in Nebuchadnezzar's dream and why we must expect God's holy angels to respond to our prayers and decrees today. We learned that the conclusion of Nebuchadnezzar's dream was that the kings of Earth must acknowledge that the Most High is sovereign over all kingdoms on Earth, and He gives them to anyone He wishes.

Does your nation acknowledge God? Do the laws in your nation favor the Church? Are the laws grounded in biblical morality?

The wars that will rage in the end times will rage against God and His holy people. Moreover, times and laws are changing; anti-God laws are increasing, and the morality of nations is at stake.

Daniel's vision doesn't mean we acquiesce to evil rule and rulers over nations as an inevitable reality. We must forcefully advance the Kingdom even though people, nations, and kings are attacking it. We must enforce Jesus' Kingdom, watching, praying, and declaring, "Thy Kingdom come, thy will be done, on Earth, as it is in heaven."

In the next chapter, we list seven more stirring reasons why we must watch, pray, and resist the spirit of slumber like never before and consider what's at stake if we don't.

CHAPTER 7: SEVEN MORE REASONS TO WATCH AND PRAY

"The wicked watches the righteous, And seeks to slay him." – King David in Psalm 37:32 NKJV

"The wicked keeps his eye on the righteous, seeking a chance to kill him." – King David in Psalm 37:32 CJB

This chapter lists additional reasons for believers to faithfully watch and pray. The first reflects the ongoing battle between the Kingdom of Heaven and the kingdom of darkness.

The wicked watch and pray.

People of all religions, including satanists, are watching and praying to their gods and spirits. The passage in Psalm 37:32 tells us that the wicked stand on their watch. They specifically keep their eye on the righteous and target them for assassination. The word used for watch in Psalm 37:32 is the same Hebrew word *tsa.phah* used in Ezekiel 3:17, where God appoints Ezekiel as a watchman, and it means to:

- look out or about, spy,
- observe, watch closely

- watch, keep watch

So, the wicked spy and closely watch the righteous. They are on their watch. Should the wicked be more committed to watching and praying than believers? The wicked watch, what about us?

This connects to our second reason. The wicked are increasing their activities.

Thieves intensify their schemes during harvest times.

Remember, Old Testament watchmen looked out over crops to protect the harvest against beasts, predators, thieves, and enemies. When thieves know the harvest is ripe (something is ready to be stolen), they increase their activities and intensify their schemes. And we know the thief comes to kill, steal, and destroy (John 10:10).

As the Lord's return gets closer, the devil intensifies his schemes. People are even inventing new ways to sin. "They are backstabbers, haters of God, insolent, proud, and boastful. They invent new ways of sinning, and they disobey their parents" (Romans 1:30 NLT). The enemy knows his time shortens with each day, so he's increasing his efforts to deceive and blind the minds of people so much so that the very elect are being deceived (Matthew 24:24, Hosea 4:6). Revelation says the devil executes his deception and destruction with anger. It says, ". . . But woe to you, land and sea, for the Adversary has come down to you, and he is very angry, because he knows that his time is short!" (Revelation 12:12 CJB).

The enemy is intensifying his tactics, and we must increase our watching and praying over the end-time harvest of souls.

We must watch against conspiracies against Israel and her ally nations.

We explored Daniel's vision in chapter 6, where an evil king speaks against the Most High, oppresses His holy people, and tries to change the set times and laws (Daniel 7:25). More conspiracies against Israel and her allies are underway. Scripture tells us to set a watch against these conspirators day and night.

> And conspired all of them together to come and to fight against Jerusalem, and to hinder it. [9] Nevertheless we made our prayer unto our God, and set a watch against them day and night, because of them. (Nehemiah 4:8-9 KJV)

As there are so many elections this year and a pivotal United States presidential election that attracts controversy and conspiracies, this Scripture confirms that we must watch and pray for the nation(s) like never before. Even if current events aren't enough

71

reason, Jesus commanded every New Testament believer to watch and pray.

Jesus commands us to watch and pray.

In chapter 4, we explored seventeen Scriptures related to New Testament watching. They establish watching and praying as every believer's responsibility because of the Lord's coming return. Jesus made it clear that we must live in expectation and anticipation of His return. We must be alert and sober, keeping our eyes open against our adversary, who is like a roaring lion seeking sleepy believers he can devour. We must stay awake. The passage in 2 Peter reminds us that the Day of the Lord will come like a thief!

> Moreover, dear friends, do not ignore this: *with the Lord, one day is like a thousand years and a thousand years like one day* [9] The Lord is not slow in keeping his promise, as some people think of slowness; on the contrary, he is patient with you; for it is not his purpose that anyone should be destroyed, but that everyone should turn from his sins. [10] *However, the Day of the Lord will come "like a thief."* On that Day the heavens will disappear with a roar, the elements will melt and disintegrate, and the earth and everything in it will be burned up. (2 Peter 3:8-10 CJB, italics added)

The only way to detect a thief is an alarm system. As watchmen, we are God's alarm system.

This passage also lets us know God transcends time. A day is like 1,000 years to Him, and 1,000 years like one day. But if we take this literally, and do the math, when Jesus asked the disciples to watch and pray for one hour, it was like asking them to watch and pray for 41 years or a generation. We are called to stand on our watch consistently throughout our generation.

We cannot pick up watching and praying and then put it down when we don't feel like it. We must continue in it, as Apostle Paul said, "Continue in prayer, and watch in the same with thanksgiving" (Colossians 4:2 KJV). Continuing or consistency is crucial.

We must be consistent in watching and praying to recognize the "running" of the watchers.

Old Testament watchmen were so consistent they could recognize who was approaching by observing their stride. They knew the running of one person from another. This is described in 2 Samuel:

> And the watchman saw another man running: and the watchman called unto the porter, and said, Behold another man running alone. And the king said, He also bringeth tidings. [27] And the watchman said, Me thinketh the running of the foremost is like the running of Ahimaaz the son of

> Zadok. And the king said, He is a good man, and cometh with good tidings. (2 Samuel 18:26-27 KJV)

Through consistency, a skilled watcher sharpens their "looking" to observe details and recognize the messengers that are coming. Remember, the watchers in Nebuchadnezzar's dream were messenger angels. We must watch and pray consistently, to the extent that we recognize the "running" (activities) of angels in response to our prayers.

We can sharpen our skills in watching and praying through consistency; the more we look, the better we can get at looking. If you don't look, you won't see. You will only find (through looking) if you refuse to give slumber to your eyelids. We must resist the spirit of slumber and not give rest to our eyelids.

We must watch and pray to resist slumber, spiritual death, and lukewarmness.

King David said, "I will not give sleep to mine eyes, or slumber to mine eyelids, *Until I find* out a place for the Lord, an habitation for the mighty God of Jacob" (Psalm 132:4-5 KJV, italics added). Watchers must discipline themselves to resist sleep and slumber. We cannot give in to the tendency of our eyelids, as David said. When the apostles' eyelids were heavy; they succumbed to the heaviness, and Jesus found them and asked, could you not watch with me for an hour?

In the same way that continued looking can lead to increased skill in watching, continued sleeping leads to blindness. Isaiah said, "His watchmen are blind: they are all ignorant, they are all dumb dogs, they cannot bark; sleeping, lying down, loving to slumber" (Isaiah 56:10 KJV). They became blind through sleeping, lying down, and loving to slumber. We must resist the spirit of slumber because it leads to blindness. Romans 11:8 says, ". . . God hath given them the spirit of slumber, eyes that they should not see, and ears that they should not hear; unto this day" (KJV).

In the same way that continued looking can lead to increased skill in watching, continued sleeping leads to blindness

---

In the Scriptures, sleeping is often used as a metaphor for death. In John 11:11, Jesus said, our friend Lazarus is asleep, and 1 Thessalonians 4:14 refers to those who have fallen asleep. The church at Sardis is described as spiritually dead. It means they were sleeping because the antidote and instruction was to wake up! God told them, ". . . you have a reputation of being alive, but you are dead. Wake up! Strengthen what remains and is about to die, for I have found your deeds unfinished in the sight of my God . . . But if you do not wake up,

I will come like a thief, and you will not know at what time I will come to you" (Revelation 3:1-3 NIV).

If we slumber, failing to watch and pray consistently, it will lead to spiritual death. We are not called to be spiritually dead or lukewarm but to be on fire. Note that one of the results of being lukewarm is blindness:

> So, because you are lukewarm—neither hot nor cold—I am about to spit you out of my mouth. [17] You say, 'I am rich; I have acquired wealth and do not need a thing.' But you do not realize that you are wretched, pitiful, poor, *blind* and naked. (Revelation 3:16-17 NIV, italics added)

The church in America must resist the deception that she is okay because of her wealth. No, God says it's possible to have material wealth and still be wretched, pitiful, poor, blind, and naked. God is not looking for a church that trusts in its material wealth. No, He is looking for a church that is hot with prayer fire—not cold.

Therefore, carefully consider the final reason we list for watching and praying.

God is counting on our watching and praying.

In the Scriptures, one of the few things God seeks is for someone to watch and pray. He said, ". . . I sought for a man among them, that should make up the hedge, and stand in the gap before me for the land, that I should not destroy it: but I found none. Therefore have I poured out mine indignation upon them; I have consumed them with the fire of my wrath: their own way have I recompensed upon their heads, saith the Lord God" (Ezekiel 22:30-31 KJV). Destruction came upon the land because no one was found to watch and pray.

God put us in charge of Earth and works in partnership with our prayers. He is counting on our prayers to avert crisis and destruction. Whatever we allow on Earth is allowed, and whatever we prohibit on Earth is prohibited (Matthew 18:18).

I pray for God's grace, discipline, and desire to watch and pray like never before. Oh Lord, give us grace and the desire to exercise the fruit of the Spirit of temperance. You work in us both to will and do your good pleasure (Philippians 2:13)!

Recap and Reflect

In this chapter, we discussed seven reasons to watch and pray:

1. The wicked watch and pray.
2. Thieves intensify their schemes during harvest times.

3. We must watch against conspiracies against Israel and her ally nations.
4. Jesus commands us to watch and pray.
5. We must be consistent in watching and praying to recognize the "running" of the watchers.
6. We must watch and pray to resist slumber, spiritual death, and lukewarmness.
7. God is counting on our watching and praying.

Which reason was most compelling to you and why? What action will you take in response?

In the next chapter, we discuss ways to take action and list prayer points for our nation(s).

CHAPTER 8: TAKE ACTION: PRAYERS FOR THE NATION

> But don't just listen to God's word. You must do what it says. Otherwise, you are only fooling yourselves. ²³ For if you listen to the word and don't obey, it is like glancing at your face in a mirror. ²⁴ You see yourself, walk away, and forget what you look like. ²⁵ But if you look carefully into the perfect law that sets you free, and if you do what it says and don't forget what you heard, then God will bless you for doing it. (James 1:22-25 NLT)

More than anything, I want to see readers act upon what is written in this book. I want us to be doers of all we have discussed concerning watching and praying. Faith without works is dead being alone (James 2:20), and we must be doers of the Word, not hearers only (James 1:22). So here are some practical ideas to ensure you begin to watch and pray like never before.

Commit to achievable, daily personal times of watching and praying.

This may seem like stating the obvious, but committing to achievable, daily individual times to watch and pray is important. Many people set unachievable goals for prayer and end up being discouraged and disappointed in themselves, leaving the door open for the enemy to attack them with guilt and condemnation. So, base your goal(s) on where you are right now.

King David gives us a biblical pattern of daily prayer to aspire to concerning our prayer goals. He said, "Evening, and morning, and at noon, will I pray, and cry aloud: and he shall hear my voice" (Psalm 55:17 KJV). Praying three times a day was his pattern, and the apostles also prayed multiple times daily. Scripture records them praying in their homes and entering the temple at the hour of prayer to pray (Acts 3:1-6).

If you don't have a consistent watch right now, start with 10 or 15 minutes two or three times a day, for example, morning and evening or morning, noon, and evening. Based on King David's pattern, our church prays weekdays at 6am, 12 noon, and 7pm. Praying just 10 minutes multiple times a day creates a prayer appetite in you that grows as you gradually increase the length and frequency of your prayers.

If you work outside your home, I also ask you to try this at least once a week. Arrive at work early—

perhaps just 10 minutes early—and watch over your office. Either sit at your desk and assess the atmosphere or slowly walk around your office to watch, assess the atmosphere, and pray in response to what you see. You can do the same with a 10-minute walk around your neighborhood or city or state capitol.

The next part of the pattern of prayer to aspire to is to increase the length to 1 hour of prayer. We know Jesus asked his sleepy disciples, "Could you not watch with me for one hour?" But if you are not already praying consistently, don't jump from zero to 360.

If you are already praying consistently for at least 30 minutes, endeavor to increase the length of your watch time to 1 hour. For example, 10 minutes of thanksgiving and worship, 20 minutes of praying in the Spirit, 10 minutes of asking God what's on His heart, waiting and watching, and in response, 20 minutes of decreeing, declaring, and praying in your understanding. That's a 10-20, 10-20 pattern to help you increase your time.

If you are already praying consistently for 1 hour, spend more time praying in the Spirit, endeavoring to hear prayer points from what the Spirit will say. Having led midnight prayer for many years, this is my approach to watching. The Spirit will help us know what to pray. Paul said, "And the Holy Spirit helps us in our weakness. For example, we don't know what God wants us to pray for. But the Holy Spirit prays for us with groanings that cannot be expressed in words" (Romans 8:26 NLT). Ask God whether you need to address a new area of prayer you have been overlooking and to reveal it to you by the Holy Spirit. I was trained to pray in the Spirit before praying in my understanding. I once had an elder from Guyana who had encountered a lot of witchcraft attacks from his background. He told me it was his custom to pray in the spirit for an hour before he prayed anything in his understanding.

At whatever level you are, to avoid disappointment, ensure your goals are:

- Specific
  - o Example: I want to watch and pray for my 1) children, 2) church, and 3) nation daily.
- Measurable
  - o Example: To begin, I will watch and pray 15 minutes a day, two times a day, 7 days a week.
- Achievable
  - o Example: I will commit to praying 15 minutes twice daily and not set an unachievable goal.
- Relevant

- o This is relevant to my preparedness for the Lord's return.
- Time-bound
  - o Example: I will achieve this goal over the next three months. I will assess my progress after three months and increase my frequency and length of prayer if I have been consistent and disciplined at this level.

Don't start with herculean goals for prayer. Start with what is achievable to ensure you gain momentum and confidence. To begin, focus on quality, not quantity or length.

To foster commitment, put daily appointments on your calendar and keep those appointments as meetings with God.

Set reminders to watch and pray on your phone, laptop, and desktop. Create screensavers and phone lock images that are reminders to watch and pray. Put a sign on your refrigerator or an index card on your bathroom mirror. Do whatever you can to encourage yourself to remain faithful to your time of watching and praying.

Continue to educate yourself about watching and praying through books like this one.

The scripture in Hosea is clear: "My people are destroyed from lack of knowledge. Because you have rejected knowledge, I also reject you as my priests; because you have ignored the law of your God, I also will ignore your children" (Hosea 4:6 NIV). Ignorance of God's Word affects us and our children. Gird yourself with sound teaching on watching, praying, and intercession. Prioritize the Bible; then, grow your library of other books on the subject. As a starter list, I include two of my books and books by other authors I have read as recommendations for your library.

I truly believe the first on the list of recommendations is necessary for all intercessors and watchers. *Fervent Fire: Understanding the Pattern of the Priesthood for Prevailing Intercessory Prayer* is the result of a vision I had years ago. I was carried out in the Spirit and saw a seething red room full of altars from my background. The book details how to deal with evil altars and the connection between the Old Testament priesthood under David and our present-day prayer watches. It provides the missing link of understanding necessary for us to be committed New Testament priests who keep the spiritual sacrifices of prayer and intercession ever-burning on our altars. Before we are intercessors, we are priests, and that reality helps us understand why we must be consistent. There is no priest without a sacrifice.

Now, here's my recommended short list of starter books about watching, praying, and intercession for your library:

- Fervent Fire: Understanding the Pattern of the Priesthood for Prevailing Intercessory Prayer by Lenita Reeves
- Understanding the Power of Agreement by Lenita Reeves
- Praying Your Loved Ones Into the Kingdom by Morris Cerullo
- The Art of Intercession by Kenneth E. Hagin
- Shaping History Through Prayer and Fasting by Derek Prince
- Enforcing Prophetic Decrees Volume 2: Prayer Watch for Community Transformation by Archbishop Nicholas Duncan-Williams
- Intercessory Prayer by Dutch Sheets
- Watchman Prayer by Dutch Sheets
- Warfare Prayer by C. Peter Wagner
- The Cry God Hears by Barbara Yoder
- Prayer that Brings Revival by David Yonggi Cho

There are many other books on watching and praying; I include these because I am familiar with them and the ministries of their authors. Whatever you read, ensure it's grounded in Scripture, and do your own research.

Also, don't just accumulate books. Set aside a weekly time to read them (at least). Choose a day when you are less busy or distracted by personal responsibilities. Remember, being a watcher requires discipline.

Join a corporate prayer watch or organization that prays for the nation(s). We provoke one another to love and good works.

Corporate times of watching and praying are necessary to exercise the power of agreement and for believers to provoke one another to love and good works. This also helps keep you accountable and connect with others of similar faith, spirit, and desire to watch and pray. For more information on our prayer watch, visit:
http://lenitareeves.org/joinprayerwatch.

The following organizations also provide resources focused on praying for America:

- American Bible Society News: 7 Ways to Pray for America
    - https://assets.news.americanbible.org/uploads/publication/National-Day-Of-Prayer-Prayer-Guide-2022.pdf
- Intercessors for America
    - https://ifapray.org/
- National Day of Prayer
    - https://www.nationaldayofprayer.org/

Again, there are others. I list these because I am familiar with their resources.

Finally, just do it. Pray for all men. Pray for those in authority. Pray for your nation.

Here are some prayer points to get started.

Prayers for our Nation(s)

Repentance on Behalf of the Nation

1. Our Father, I repent on behalf of our nation and ask for forgiveness for our nation's sins and healing from the consequences thereof. In the name of Jesus, let your kingdom come to my nation, and for the sake of the remnant, let any reproach over my nation be turned into a blessing.
    a. **Proverbs 14:34 NKJV:** Righteousness exalts a nation, But
        sin is a reproach to any people.

Prayers of Protection from Attacks and Conspiracies

1. According to Genesis 18:26, Lord have mercy on America for the sake of the righteous remnant. In the name of Jesus, I cancel evil projections and programmings in the womb of time to bring surprise attacks, unforeseen

crises, or winds of destruction against my nation.

   a. **Genesis 18:26 NKJV:** So the LORD said, "If I find in Sodom fifty righteous within the city, then I will spare all the place for their sakes."

2. I declare there will be no bloodshed or civil unrest over the next national election. Let any evil day of destruction the enemy wants to bring to my nation be overturned, and let the opposite occur.

   a. **Esther 9:1 NKJV:** Now in the twelfth month, that *is*, the month of Adar, on the thirteenth day, *the time* came for the king's command and his decree to be executed. On the day that the enemies of the Jews had hoped to overpower them, the opposite occurred, in that the Jews themselves overpowered those who hated them.

3. I declare evil conspiracies, and any plot of terror against my nation is exposed and canceled.

   a. **Psalm 64:2 NIV:** Hide me from the conspiracy of the wicked, from the plots of evildoers.

Prayers of Protection from Plagues and Pandemics

1. I stand on the promise of protection from evil diseases for my life, family, church, and

nation. I declare deliverance from any pestilence (plague or pandemic).

    a. **Psalm 91:3-6 KJV:** Surely he shall deliver thee from the snare of the fowler, and from the noisome pestilence. [4] He shall cover thee with his feathers, and under his wings shalt thou trust: his truth shall be thy shield and buckler. [5] Thou shalt not be afraid for the terror by night; nor for the arrow that flieth by day; [6] Nor for the pestilence that walketh in darkness; nor for the destruction that wasteth at noonday.

    b. **Psalm 91:3-6 NLT:** For he will rescue you from every trap and protect you from deadly disease. [4] He will cover you with his feathers. He will shelter you with his wings. His faithful promises are your armor and protection. [5] Do not be afraid of the terrors of the night, nor the arrow that flies in the day. [6] Do not dread the disease that stalks in darkness, nor the disaster that strikes at midday.

2. Lord, I pray that you divinely intervene and bring deliverance to the nation from any reoccurrence of COVID-19 or any new plague for the sake of the remnant.

a. **Genesis 18:23-26 KJV:** And Abraham drew near, and said, Wilt thou also destroy the righteous with the wicked? 24 Peradventure there be fifty righteous within the city: wilt thou also destroy and not spare the place for the fifty righteous that are therein? 25 That be far from thee to do after this manner, to slay the righteous with the wicked: and that the righteous should be as the wicked, that be far from thee: Shall not the Judge of all the earth do right? 26 And the Lord said, If I find in Sodom fifty righteous within the city, then I will spare all the place for their sakes.

3. In the name of Jesus, I declare that as I, your royal priest intercede, any pending plague is stayed.

a. **Numbers 16:46-48 KJV:** And Moses said unto Aaron, Take a censer, and put fire therein from off the altar, and put on incense, and go quickly unto the congregation, and make an atonement for them: for there is wrath gone out from the Lord; the plague is begun. 47 And Aaron took as Moses commanded, and ran into the midst of the congregation; and, behold, the plague was begun among the people:

and he put on incense, and made an atonement for the people. ⁴⁸ And he stood between the dead and the living; and the plague was stayed.

4. I declare that the blood of Jesus covers my movements. I plead the blood of Jesus over the communities, towns, cities, states, and nations I travel through. I declare that the destruction will not enter but pass over.

   a. **Exodus 12:22-23 KJV:** And ye shall take a bunch of hyssop, and dip it in the blood that is in the bason, and strike the lintel and the two side posts with the blood that is in the bason; and none of you shall go out at the door of his house until the morning. ²³ For the Lord will pass through to smite the Egyptians; and when he seeth the blood upon the lintel, and on the two side posts, the Lord will pass over the door, and will not suffer the destroyer to come in unto your houses to smite you.

Prayer Against Evil Bills, Laws, Decrees

1. I pray that no bill or law will be passed to disadvantage the Church or the needy. I overturn evil decrees, bills, and laws, in Jesus' name.

a. **Isaiah 10:1-2 KJV:** Woe unto them that decree unrighteous decrees, and that write grievousness which they have prescribed; [2] To turn aside the needy from judgment, and to take away the right from the poor of my people, that widows may be their prey, and that they may rob the fatherless!

2. I pray that no bill or law will be passed that facilitates the destruction of God's people, but let bills that favor God's righteous cause be passed in Jesus' name.

a. **Esther 3:8-9 NIV:** Then Haman said to King Xerxes, "There is a certain people dispersed among the peoples in all the provinces of your kingdom who keep themselves separate. Their customs are different from those of all other people, and they do not obey the king's laws; it is not in the king's best interest to tolerate them. [9] If it pleases the king, let a decree be issued to destroy them, and I will give ten thousand talents of silver to the king's administrators for the royal treasury."

Prayers for Leaders

1. In the name of Jesus, I declare that our city, town, county, state, and national leaders move with wisdom and urgency regarding issues that affect us.

    a. **1 Timothy 2:1-2 KJV:** I exhort therefore, that, first of all, supplications, prayers, intercessions, and giving of thanks, be made for all men; 2 For kings, and for all that are in authority; that we may lead a quiet and peaceable life in all godliness and honesty.

2. In Jesus' name, I pray that our leaders would be surrounded by godly counsel and those who have advanced knowledge from the Holy Ghost, like Joseph, who had advanced knowledge about the seven years of plenty and famine.

    a. **Genesis 41:25-27 KJV:** And Joseph said unto Pharaoh, The dream of Pharaoh is one: God hath shewed Pharaoh what he is about to do. 26 The seven good kine are seven years; and the seven good ears are seven years: the dream is one. 27 And the seven thin and ill favoured kine that came up after them are seven years; and the seven empty ears blasted with the east wind shall be seven years of famine.

3. Lord, I pray that righteous, God-fearing leaders would arise in our nation, in Jesus' name.

   a. **Proverbs 29:2 NIV:** When the godly are in authority, the people rejoice. But when the wicked are in power, they groan.

4. I pray that our leaders will not be selfish, self-centered, or worried about being politically correct in this hour but will make the righteous decisions necessary to save lives, in Jesus' name.

Prayers for All

1. I pray for myself and for the body of Christ for desire to be persistent in prayer. Persistence breaks the resistance! Lord, please work in us to have the desire and strength to watch and pray consistently.

   a. **Psalm 55:17 KJV:** Evening, and morning, and at noon, will I pray, and cry aloud: and he shall hear my voice.

   b. **Philippians 2:13 KJV:** For it is God which worketh in you both to will and to do of his good pleasure.

2. I cry out for compassion for the lost. I ask you Father for desire and hunger to see souls

saved.

- a. **1 John 3:17 KJV:** But whoso hath this world's good, and seeth his brother have need, and shutteth up his bowels of compassion from him, how dwelleth the love of God in him?

3. Father, I put You in remembrance of Your promise; You are not willing that any should perish. I cry out for my unsaved loved ones, co-workers, and neighbors to come to the place of repentance.

- a. **2 Peter 3:9 NKJV:** The Lord is not slack concerning *His* promise, as some count slackness, but is longsuffering toward us, not willing that any should perish but that all should come to repentance.

4. I intercede for my unsaved family members. Father, I ask You to remove the scales and blinders from their eyes and for Your goodness to lead them to repentance in Jesus' name.

- a. **Acts 26:18 KJV:** To open their eyes, and to turn them from darkness to light, and from the power of Satan unto God, that they may receive forgiveness of sins, and inheritance among them which are sanctified by faith that is in me.

5. I take authority over territorial spirits and the powers of darkness that want to block the release of souls and blind them to the gospel. I

declare a harvest of souls flows into the Church.

    a. **2 Corinthians 4:3-4 KJV:** But if our gospel be hid, it is hid to them that are lost: 4 In whom the god of this world hath blinded the minds of them which believe not, lest the light of the glorious gospel of Christ, who is the image of God, should shine unto them.

6. Holy Spirit, I ask You to show me specifically how to minister to each member of my family—whether I should **"be merciful to those who doubt; save others by snatching them from the fire; [or] show mercy, mixed with fear" according to Jude 1:23.** Holy Spirit, reveal opportunities to share the Good News, and give me the strength to obey when You open the door.

    a. **Jude 1:22-23 KJV:** And of some have compassion, making a difference: 23 And others save with fear, pulling them out of the fire; hating even the garment spotted by the flesh.

    b. **Jude 1:22-23 NIV:** Be merciful to those who doubt; 23 save others by snatching them from the fire; to others show mercy, mixed with fear—hating even the clothing stained by corrupted flesh.

7. I declare that multitudes of souls will be added to the Church according to Acts 5:14.

        c. **Acts 5:14 KJV:** And more than ever believers were added to the Lord, multitudes of both men and women.

8. Lord, I pray You will be lifted up in my life and the Church in every way and that You will draw souls to Yourself.

        d. **John 12:32 KJV:** "And I, when I am lifted up from the earth, will draw all people to myself."

9. I declare that the Lord will increase the Church with men like a flock and multiply the Church through new souls saved.

        e. **Ezekiel 36:37 KJV:** Thus saith the Lord God; I will yet for this be enquired of by the house of Israel, to do it for them; I will increase them with men like a flock.

Conclusion

It's time to act; it's time to watch and pray like never before. As New Testament believers, it's our responsibility to watch and pray. God put us in charge and gave us authority. Old Testament watchers give us insight to watch over harvests, city walls, and God's people. With the Holy Spirit's help, we can climb the watchtower in prayer and declare what we see and hear. We are God's alarm system.

Several New Testament Scriptures command us to watch and pray, not because we are prophets but because of the Lord's return and the events that will precede it. We must legislate and decree God's decrees through prayer and expect His holy angels to respond to our prayers. The wicked are on their watch; what about us? We must resist the spirit of slumber. Let's take action and watch and pray for our families, leaders, and nation(s) like never before!

About the Author

Rev. Lenita Reeves is an apostle-prophet by ascension gift and has traveled to nations to preach the gospel. She serves as the senior pastor of Action Chapel Baltimore and Action Chapel North Carolina churches under the covering of Archbishop Nicholas Duncan-Williams, who ordained her into ministry. She is the founder of the APT Apostolic and Prophetic Women Network, Prayer Watch with Pastor Lenita, School of Intercession: Altar vs. Altar, PurposeHouse Biblical Counseling, and PurposeHouse Publishing, and has been leading midnight prayer watch for over two decades.

She is the author of several books, including *Fervent Fire: Understanding the Pattern of the Priesthood for Prevailing Intercessory Prayer* and *Understanding the Power of Agreement: A Necessary Key for Prayer, Relationships, and Progress.* She has over twenty years of Christian teaching experience and over ten years of professional, corporate instructional design experience. She has also served as an adjunct faculty member and teacher trainer.

As an abuse survivor and former teen mom, God has graced Lenita to be an outspoken overcomer, sharing her testimony freely and, as a result, seeing captives set free all over the world. She is an international conference speaker, a member of the RAINN speaker's bureau, and has traveled the world to conduct apostolic missions and train leaders in London, Liberia, Jamaica, Haiti, the Bahamas, Kenya, Uganda, and Ghana.

She began her service to the Lord in campus ministry. As Deputy Director of Campus Ministries United, she was pivotal in planting campus branches and coordinating an annual conference to bring various campus ministries together in a night of prayer, praise, and relationship building. In the next phase of her ministry, God taught her the basics of pastoring while serving as a youth minister. She later served as a prophetic intercessory leader and assistant pastor, gathering believers for fasting and prayer. And prayer and intercession still undergird the apostolic and prophetic grace of her ministry.

She speaks with transparency, highlighting her highs as well as her lows to show others that God can turn pain into a platform and use the foolish things of this world to confound the wise. From senior class president to director in Corporate America to founder of a non-profit and pastor, leadership has been an evident mark of Lenita's life calling and passions. She is Bishop Bill Hamon/Christian International Authorized Prophetic Instructor and graduate of the Christian International School of Prophets. She has a BS in Industrial Engineering from Georgia Tech, an MA in Dance Education from the Ohio State University, and an MBA from the University of

Maryland, College Park. She attended Beulah Heights Bible College in Atlanta, Georgia, then under Dr. Sam Chand's leadership, and is currently a doctoral candidate in Christian Counseling. Lenita was ordained in Action Chapel International in Ghana by Archbishop Nicholas Duncan-Williams and in Action Chapel North America. She resides in Maryland with her family.

For more information, visit www.lenitareeves.org.

Other Titles

- *Fervent Fire: Understanding the Pattern of the Priesthood for Prevailing Intercessory Prayer*
- *Understanding the Power of Agreement: A Necessary Key for Prayer, Relationships, and Progress*
- *The Spirit of Rejection: Heal its wounds, Restore your Self-Esteem, and Move on to Promotion*
- *Breaking the Silence: The Journey from Rape to Redemption*
- *An Anchor for My Soul: Soul-stabilizing Devotions for the Multi-tasked Woman*

Stay Connected

Discover the latest tools and encouragement for living on purpose! Visit www.lenitareeves.org and join our mailing list for the latest blog posts, continued news, and previews of other upcoming books.

Visit us on Social Media
Facebook/ Instagram/ TikTok/ YouTube:
@pastorlenita

Online Courses

- *School of Intercession 101: The Priesthood of Intercession*
- *School of Intercession 102: Activating Spiritual Gifts for Targeted Intercession*
- *Now Discover Purpose: 80 Days to Stop Wondering, Unleash Your Purpose Design and Create a 365-Day Plan to Live on Purpose*
- *How to Teach the Bible with Excellence: Answering the Call to the Teaching Ministry*
- *APT Company: Six-month Mentoring for the Apostolic and Prophetic Mandates*